Portrait of Flowers

Dianne E. Woods

DEDICATION

I dedicate this book to my family and friends who have supported me throughout the years in all my endeavors. Love you all!

PORTRAITS

Authors Note

With our hearts and minds constantly on the move, there can be no time to sit and be still. *Portrait of Flowers* is solely printed to bring that moment in time you may have missed by the business of life. I selected the word Portrait instead of picture to note that everything has a purpose, or a story. Think about it, the detail that goes into every creation. Do you really stop to smell the roses? Have you ever taken occasion to wonder about a flower, its purpose, or life span? Most can say "not really" because we're stressed, overworked, and totally distracted by "life." When I take a minute to get up close and emerge myself in the beauty of nature, I am totally energized. That's my experience. We're all fashioned to have and live our own experience, and no two are, or can ever be identical.

The takeaway from this publication is simply what you desire it to be. Use your imagination to see the beauty, or not. The perception of a thing is important to how we respond. The short story accompanying the portrait has nothing to do with the flower, its species, or intended to be factual. Smell, touch, sight, hear, and taste make up humanities five senses, but that's not all. Emotions, and our mental state, play a huge part in actions and reactions. Perception is everything, and dictates judgements about the world we live in. We can totally manipulate these senses to please, and if you don't think so, ask someone to take a picture. Regardless of their attitude at that split second, they break into a smile for the pictures sake, look "happy," and afterwards return to the "previous" attitude once the photo is taken. *Portrait of Flowers* purpose is to show there is more to everything than the first impression. Explore details in each portrait, there's always something new to discover. Enjoy!

Dianne E. Woods

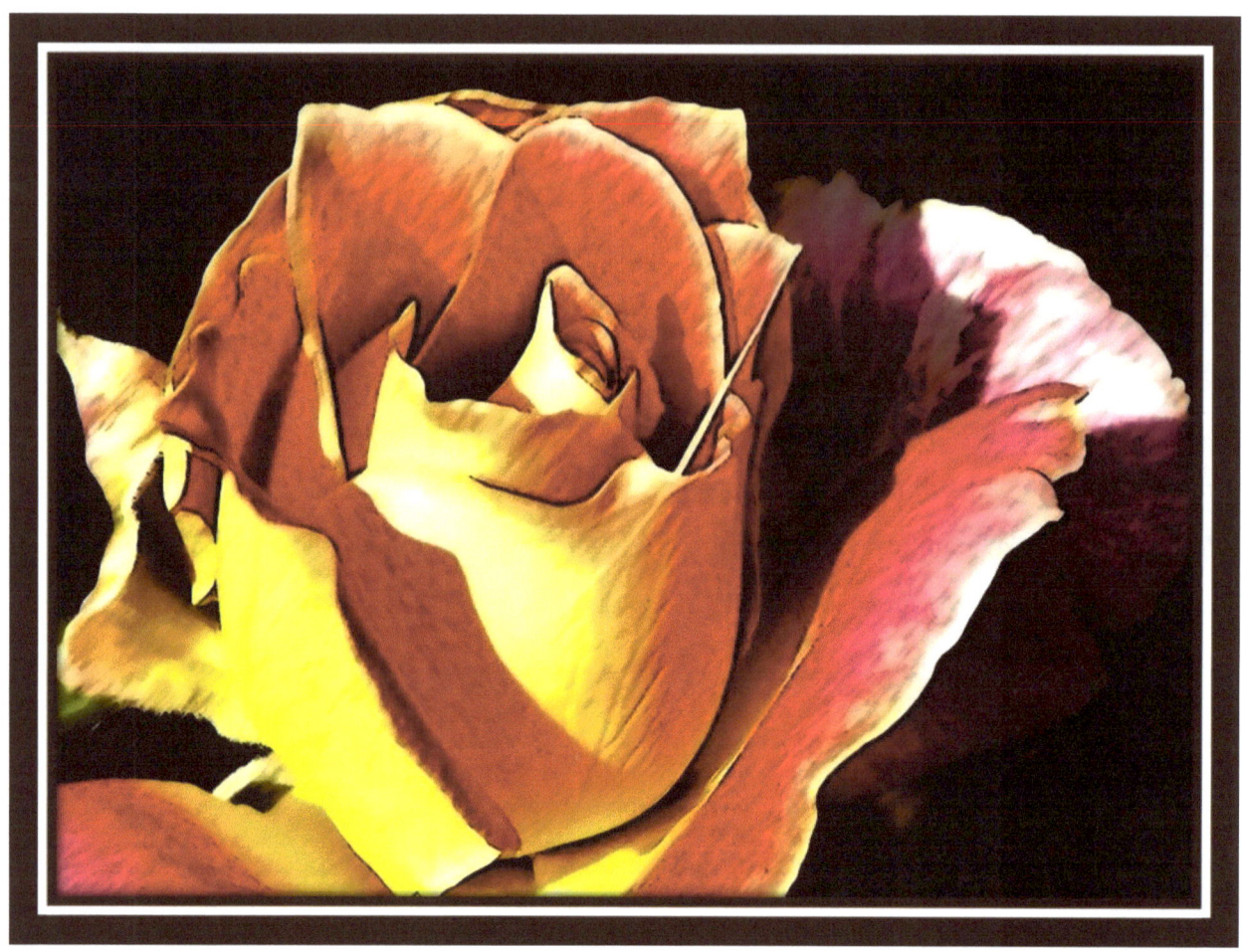

COLOR'S GALORE [Paint Stokes]

Color's Galore! That's who I am. Although rough around the edges, I love to show off my abundant hues of pink, orange, yellow, and white, as they fade like mountain waterfalls seamlessly into one another. Notwithstanding my firm soldier style stem, dressed in its army green, secures me tightly at attention as the wind bends me from side to side. It's hot today, and one of my petals is scorched, and withered, can you see it? Not at all like the best parts of me, those lines weaving through my petals pointing upward to strengthen and keep me fresh, as moisture from the dew rinses me off during my morning shower. It's not enough! It is so hot! Have you ever been so hot you change colors? It may not be yellow, but possibly red, pink, or flush. What makes you change colors? The colors of your personality or emotions that is. I know my colors are natural, created for me by God, but I think I would be much happier if that ugly petal wasn't there. Did you know your personality and emotions are like the colors of my petals that fade seamlessly into one another, created by God, specifically unique to you? Is it natural to wish them away, see them as ugly, or allow them to lose their purpose to please yourself or others? As I surge through my life cycle, I see thousands of eyes that gaze upon me when visitors stroll through the garden where I'm planted. They do nothing to help me with the heat, and ignore the ugly part of my makeup. "Withered and scorched petal, I wish you would blow away. If you didn't exist I would be unspoiled!" Hmmm, do I really believe I could be unspoiled, or is my focus on what I perceive as ugly make me feel less colorful? Do you feel that way about parts of you screaming to be, or not to be acknowledge? I need to change my thinking. What part of you seems unpleasant in your awareness of you? If it were gone, would it really make a difference in who you are? People stop by, watch me grow, and I wish they would remove that part of me I don't like. They don't see what I feel about me, but there's a sign posted at the entrance of the garden, like the entrance of the garden of your heart that says "Do Not Touch." Rats!

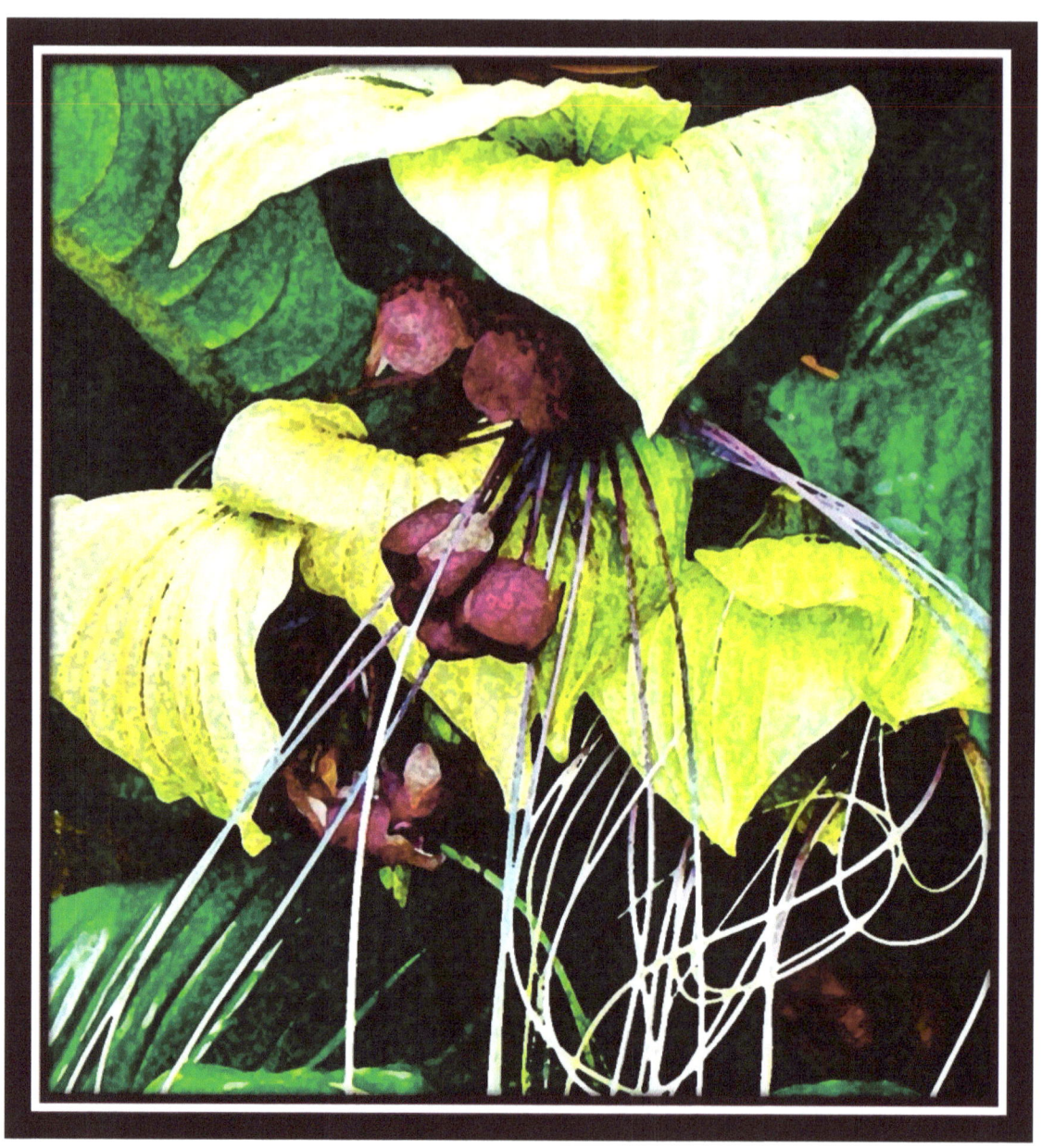

COMPUTER CORDS [Water Color Sponge]

Yeowee! I got everything plugged in, finally! How many times have I done this? Organize, reorganize, plug in, unplug, or untangle. It's an endless cycle people! There's a cord for every part of me that has a definite purpose, but I get so tired of always trying to keep things straight. It would be nice to organize these cords once and be done with it. If I disconnect one, or another gradually loosens without my knowledge, my entire life's rhythm becomes dysfunctional, and I start to wither and become frustrated. My cords serve not only to bring uniqueness to my beauty, but nourish me 24/7, maintain the purple in my pedals, and myriad of green shades in my leaves. I can't live without them. In your life there are cords for every part, they have a definite purpose, and you can't live without them. Cords that God has designed to connect you to your physical beauty and creativity. Cords to nourish your body, and cords of relationships to feed the spirit and soul. Organize, reorganize, plug in, unplug, or untangle it *is* an endless cycle! You know what I mean. As much as you love peace and tranquility, dysfunctional, loosened, or unplugged cords can cause stress, or a sense of being out of sync, isolated, or lonely. Your cords must be nourished and maintained. Nourishment and maintenance of your personal "computer cords," takes an awareness of who you are, God's presence in your life, and where your journey is taking you. There will always be seasons of change. Like the computer cord which keeps electricity flowing from the source to its components, you must monitor every situation, organize, reorganize, plug in, unplug, or untangled each relationship, as it presents itself. It's inevitable, takes time, and yes my friend, an "Endless Untangling Cycle!"

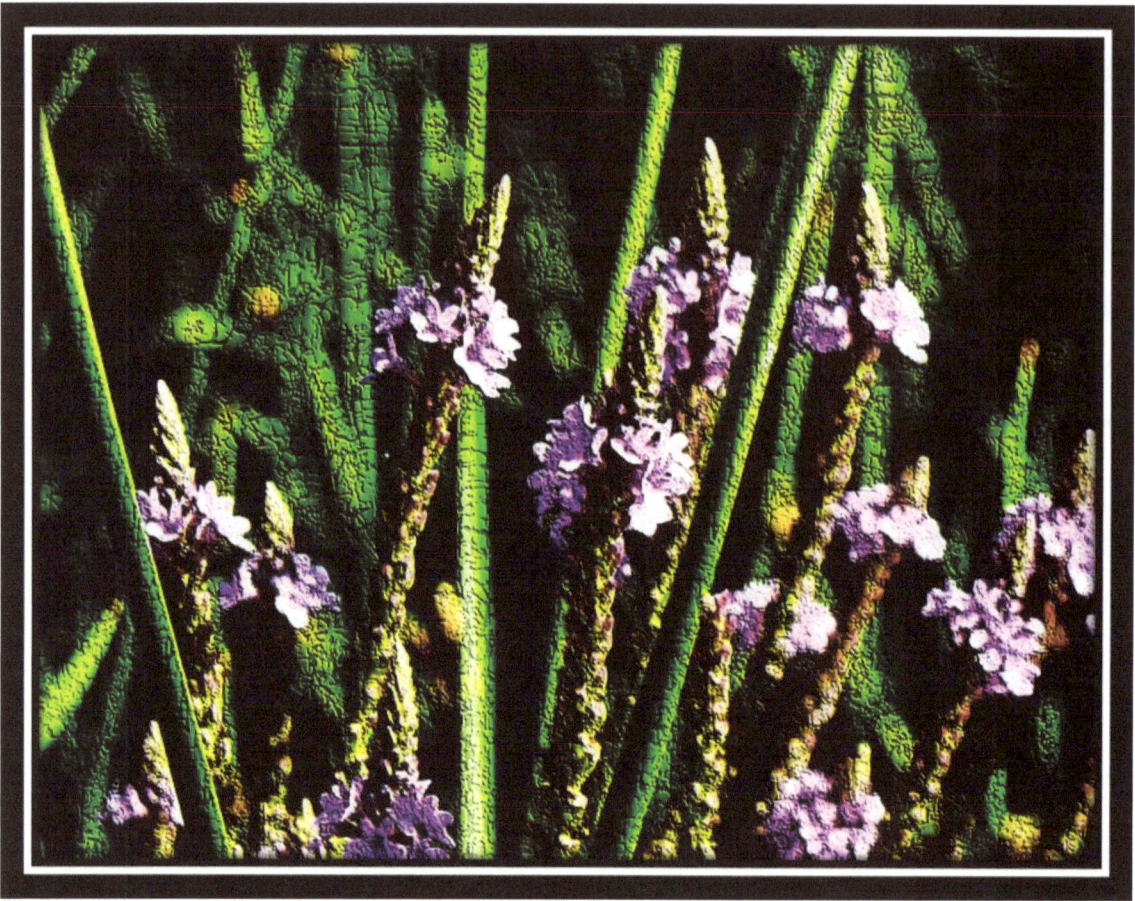

CHOIR [Cement]

Unison? I don't think so! We're the Choir of Many Voices. We usually hear from the Conductor, as he wraps his stem on the trunk of a nearby tree in an effort to bring order, "We must be in unison!" Not this choir. You see, we're the Choir of Many Voices, and we must sing louder, compete, and outshine each other with our ability. We all can make those special musical runs in order to get noticed. Not one of us wants to end up being silenced by the voice next to us, or never getting that oh so coveted solo. "Hear me! La la la la." "No, hear me! Me, may, my, mo, moo." My voice has to be louder than my neighbor, after all I have more purple blooms, I'm taller, my green stalks are stronger, well rounded, without blemish, and of course I have new blooms waiting to burst at the seams on top. It's chaos here in this Choir. Too many voices trying to be heard at once and nobody is listening. "Choir, choir!" the Conductor shouts. How can he lead, being one of us? Well, I'm at the point of exhaustion. Too many voices, and finally with help from the Conductor, we all begin to quiet down, listen, and calm our competitive natures. I understand. It can be similar with you. To make your voice matter, your opinions important to someone other than yourself, can feel chaotic when you realize there is no one to listen. Planning what to say before the other finishes their thought, takes on a competitive nature from within, "I can't wait to give my opinion about..." rolls around in your head. God has given you creative ideas and the ability to communicate effectively, and sometimes you have to work with the Choir, and other times it's a solo. Your mind is the conductor of your thoughts, but God is the Conductor of your spirit. Constantly He taps on the tree trunk of your spirit to get your attention "listen" instead of "engage." We the Choir of Many Voices urge you to think in terms of unison as you communicate with others, including yourself. Calm your thoughts and spirit long enough to hear with full attention to what is being said inside and out. Your voice does matter, and there are many ways to be heard. "Can I Get a Witness?"

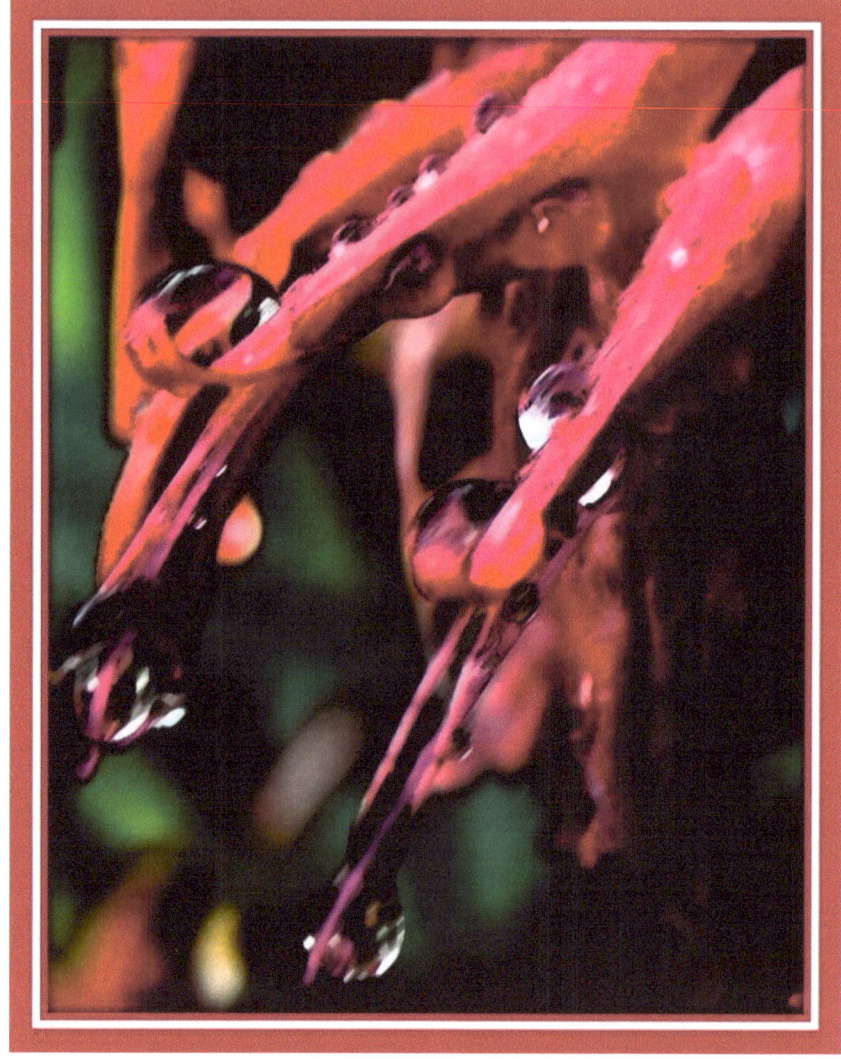

HOLD ON [Paint Strokes]

Hold on guys! I want to make sure my team knows it's not over until the job is done. What job you ask? The cycle of our purpose. See I'm a dew drop in charge of all the other dew drops assigned to this flower until the sun rises, and we're dried out by the heat and light of day. I'm the heftiest drop up top in the lip of the largest petal. Can you find me? Held in place by my appointed leaf, my pH balance and moisture levels are perfect. When I appear for my shift before sunrise I know my objective, and those of my team, which is to revive, refresh, and rejuvenate this flower from the dryness of the previous day. In addition, by example, I inspire the other dew drops to remain in place, and hold on until our purpose is complete. Some abandon their assignment early, sliding off, and landing in the dirt below making adjustment to their original aim. Others abort their assignment immediately pretending to be rain falling from the sky. The goal is to stay in place, and live out each individual journey. I want you to know that God yearns for you to live in purpose, on purpose. It's not over. You have what it takes to complete the assignment. Your dreams, ideas, creativity and desires are like my fellow dew drops, all have a specific purpose which can be achieved. Hold on! Struggle is required. "Circumstances beyond your control," you chant, those can unknowingly be part of the task, however, not the bad stuff. It's how you regulate, respond, and react on the natural side. It's how you revive, refresh, and rejuvenate on the spiritual side. Hold on! Listen and respond to God's plan for your life. You know it comes from the inside out, and energizes your every step. Do your best to not slide off the petal of your journey by the opinions of others. Resist self-doubt, the abortionist of dreams and ideas, which cause your desires and creativity to fall like rain from the sky into the dirt of disappointment. These hazards steal your original ambitions of being… or having…! It's not over. "Hold on! You *Can* Do It!"

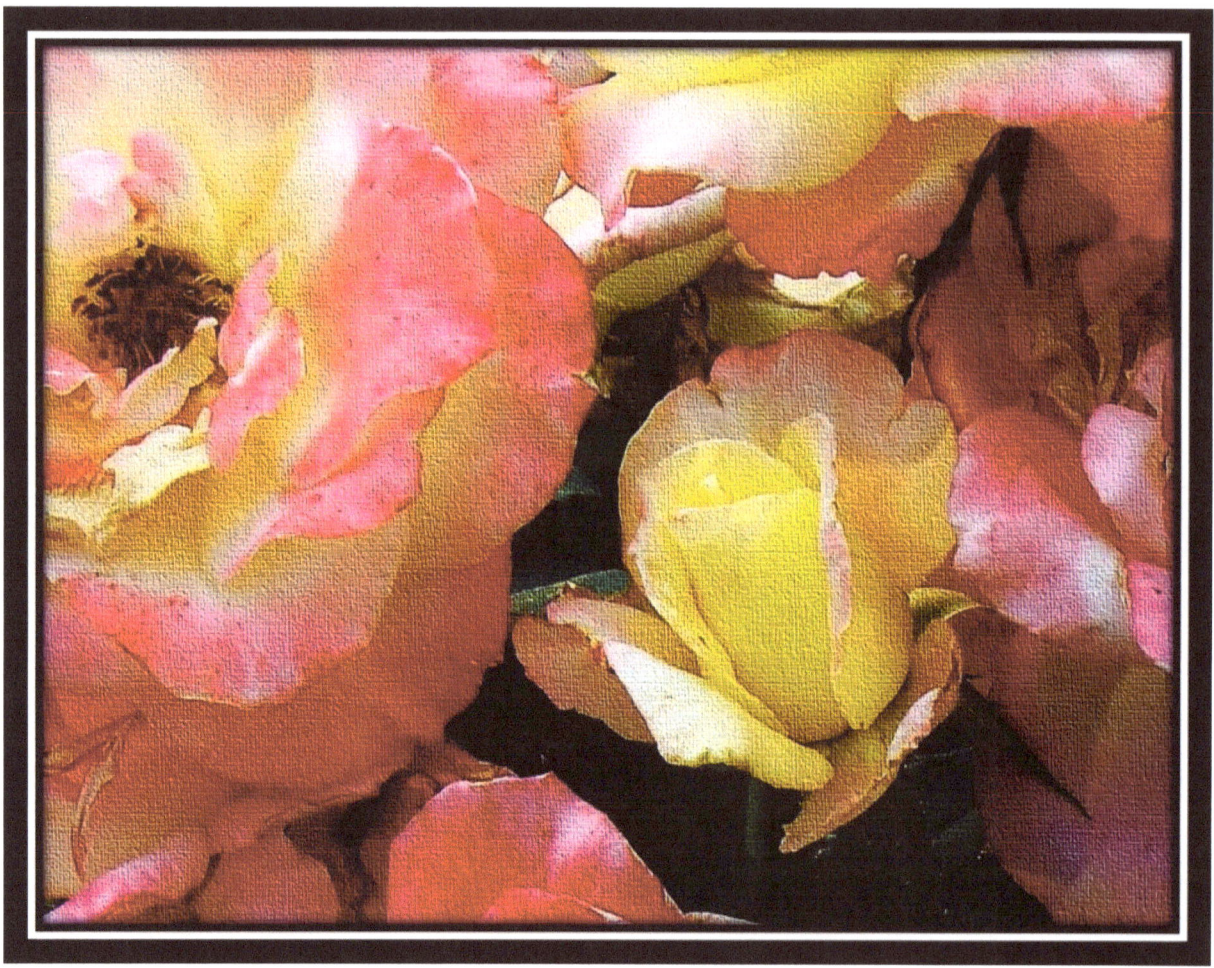

INFLUENCERS [Texturizer]

Who am I? I know who I'm supposed to be. Beginning this journey among so much maturity, everybody has an opinion. These are the influencers. Be this, do that, act like me, live this way, it's so confusing. Who am I? I really don't see myself in any influencers which surround me. This is where I am planted, however, the pressure to conform is crushing me. My assignment is distinct. My life cycle and purpose created by God is to live within my uniqueness. How can I get the Influencers to understand it is impossible to be like them? I know who I am. I know what I was created to do. I'm one created with colors of yellow and pink never to be apportioned to another. Insects appointed to feed from my nectar have never passed this way before. My quarter-inch thorny stems, and spiny green leaves, cause me to grow to a specific height prescribed only to me. Why oh, why do Influencers want to change me? I guess it's the same reason influencers want to change you. Ask yourself, "Who am I?" Who are the influencers in my life? Have I lost myself in the midst of the influencers?" Some good, some bad, but really their dreams and desires are taken from what they see on the surface of your life, their personal world view, and not your God given purpose. I had to withstand. It's not to say they're not good influencers, but when they move you away from your appointed destiny in order to control your journey, you need to stand firm. Only you know what's going on inside. Personality, likes, dislikes, abilities, dreams and desires, your uniqueness hidden deep within, the "real" you never emerges. Don't live this way. You are wonderfully created with a specific calling all your own. Influencers think they know what's best, use their wisdom to guide, but not control the matchlessness of your being. "Do You with No Regrets!"

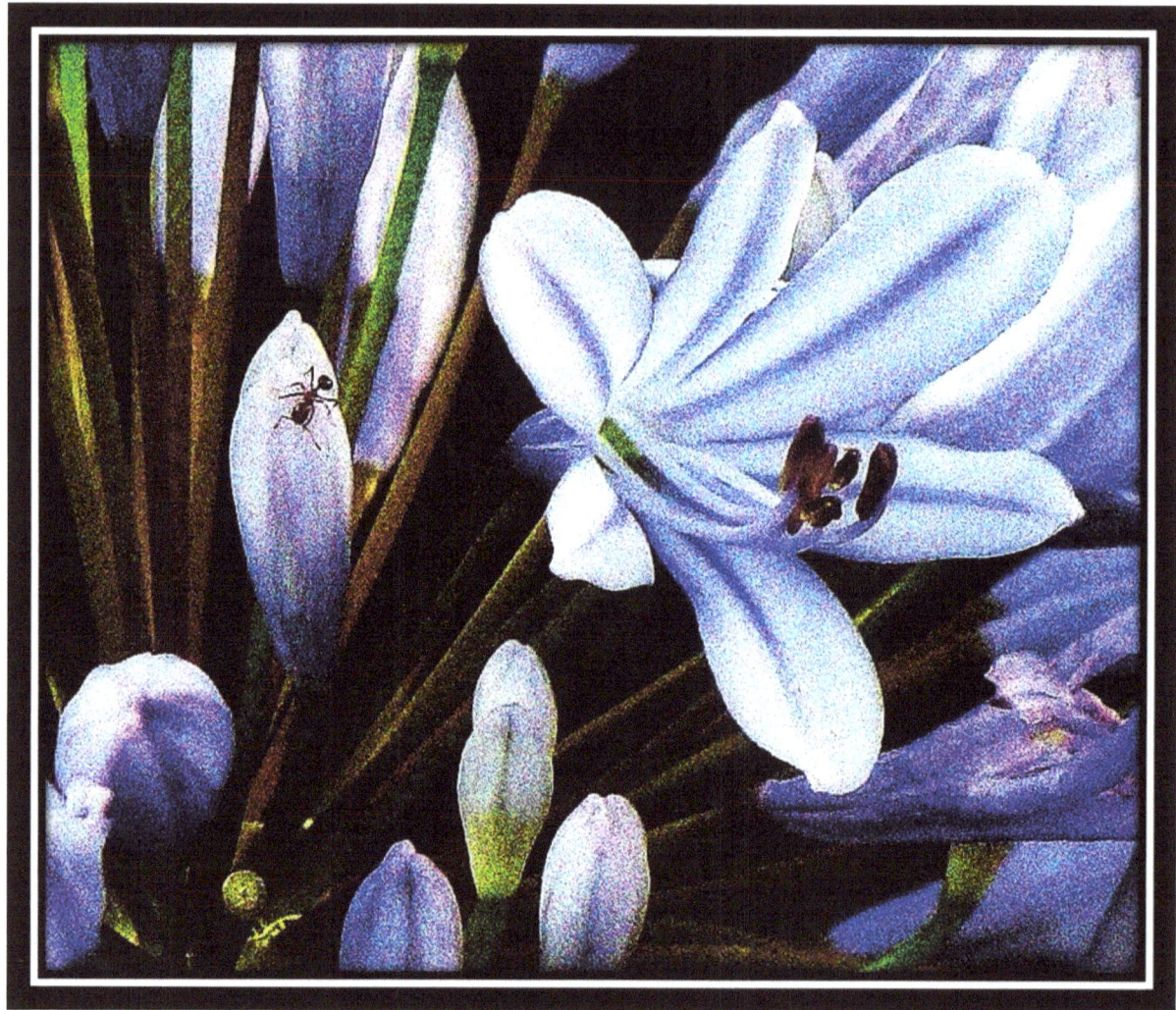

GUESSING GAME [Film Grain]

What is he thinking? This ant must have something on its mind. Probably thinking about how to get into the sweet nectar of my core. "Ah ha," too far away, and it's a big fall if he plans to leap. Probably thinking about why he chose the stem of a closed pedal instead of my other luscious, fully extended, blue and white trumpet blossoms, with ski slope tentacles cascading from my center. It would have been much easier to move around if he made a better choice. I know, he's thinking about lunch, his buddies, what to tell the Queen when he has to make excuses for a failed adventure. Maybe he's not thinking about any of my presumptions. After all, I can't read his mind, and my idea of what he's thinking are probably 100% wrong. "Hey what you thinking

Mr. Ant." "Oh I'm thinking about my family, what an awesome sight from the top of this unopened blossom, and how I wish they were here to experience the beauty of my view." Yikes! I totally misinterpreted his thoughts and actions. How about you? Is assuming another's thoughts by facial expressions, or outward circumstances a regular part of your lifestyle? Many call it "judging." It's in your nature to be curious, nonetheless you're probably wrong. Until something is verbally communicated it's not such a good idea to play mind, or face reader. Negativity wreaks havoc with these types of actions, and can take you down the pathway of annoyance wasting precious emotional energy. What would happen if you asked, instead of allowing the racetrack of your thoughts to take you to the land of assumption, and presumption? I bet you were thinking, "Is that ant really on the petal, or did the photographer place it there for special effect?" Oops, there I go again. What were you thinking about this photograph at first glance? The ant *is* really a part of the original photograph captured at a moment in time. On that note, I'm going to stop the guessing game and ask before I interpret, "What's on Your Mind?"

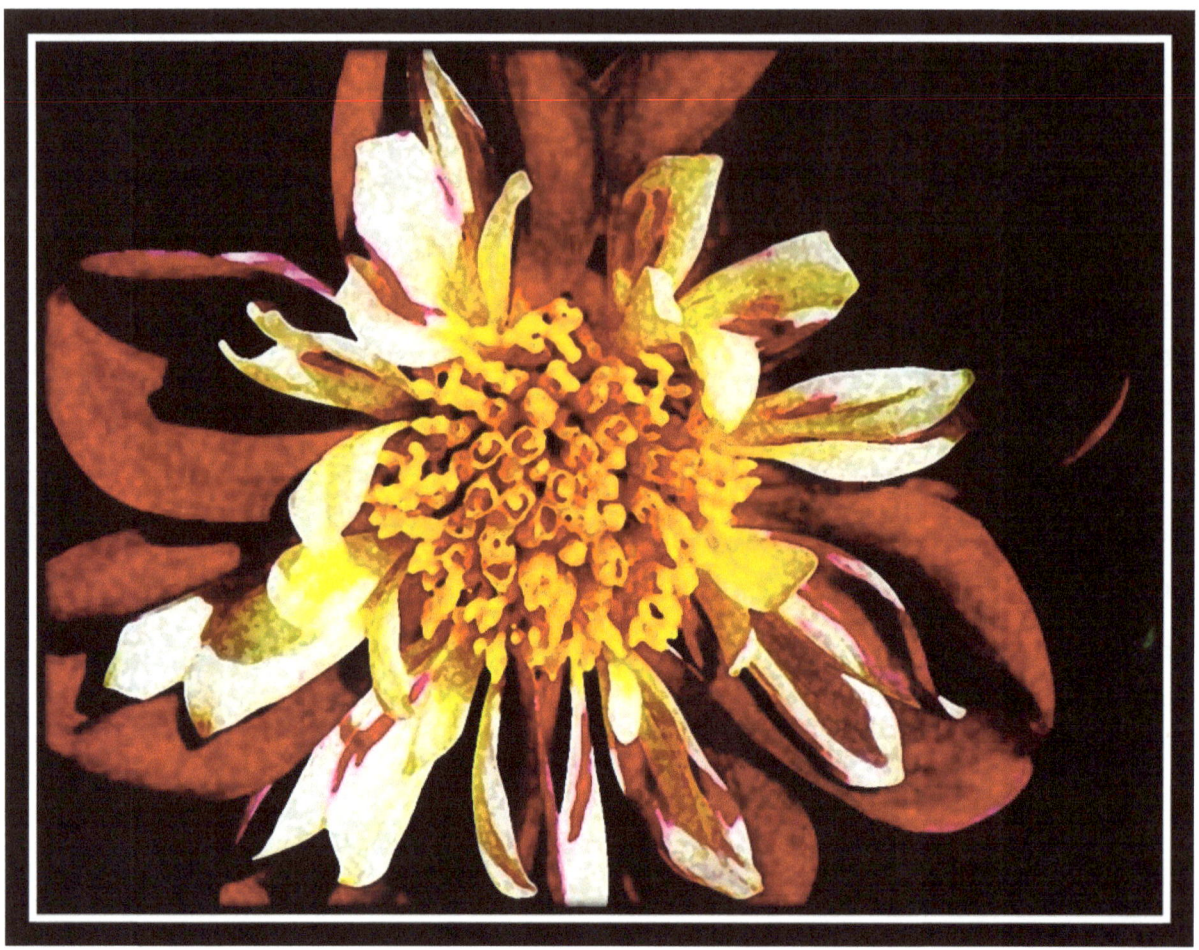

MIXED MESSAGES [Water Color Sponge]

Tulip says I'm giving off mixed messages about my species color. She says she can't figure out whether I'm supposed to be yellow, brown, red, white, pink, gold, or fuchsia. Does it matter? Occasionally it hurts to experience the questioning gawks, like I don't know my own identity. I guess if I were majority yellow, I could fit in with the Sunflowers, or red with the Roses. Maybe if I were all white I could pass as a Lily, or all pink, a Posey. "I am what I am, Tulip." "Well when asked your color on the planting instructions, what do you select?" "I select all the boxes because I can. I'm special like that. It's a privilege. There are no mixed messages here, only a lack of understanding on your part. I never pretend to be the flower I was not created by God to be. I walk in the fullness of my beauty and don't concern myself when others try to guess my species color." Maybe this has happened to you. Have people ever accused you of giving off mixed messages? "What are you?" is usually the opening line referring to your ethnicity. Those wondering glares and stares. You can't be anything other than what you were created to be. No matter the exterior color the foundation is the same. You can't breathe without oxygen, you can't live without a heartbeat. It's not your issue, it's theirs. Affirmation is important to most, but know that you are already affirmed by God. He created and equipped you with everything needed to prosper in your own skin. Taking on emotionally the attitudes of others drags you down unnecessarily. Select all the boxes if need be. Keep moving. It's an option only granted to those who qualify. Under no circumstances allow the sentiments of others to question your identity, or make you wish you were someone you could never be. There is no such thing as mixed messages only misinterpretations. "Stay True Be You."

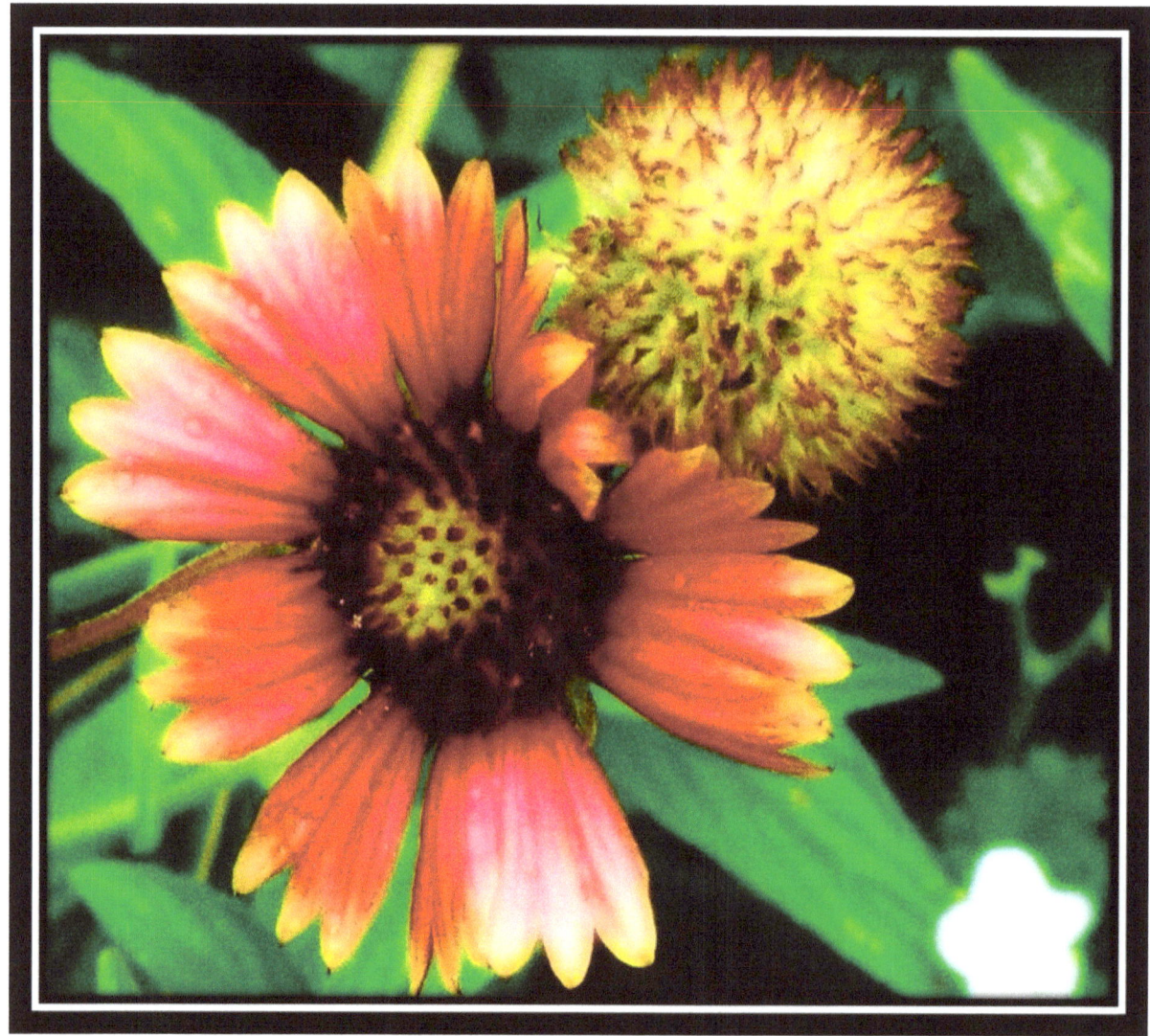

MISSING LINK [Glow Diffuse]

I can't believe they left so early? It would be nice to be fully arrayed without missing one petal. What can I do? Not much. Gaps create a missing link, but they don't change the end purpose. Adaptation it's critical. When petal fell to the sand I thought I was weakened. Not so. I realized it's only an opportunity to adjust to a new way to complete my intended purpose. They said they would stick with me through thick and thin. Promises, promises. It's only a problem if I allow. I learned quickly that God was the gap in what I considered a missing link. Still beautiful, still functional, still able to fulfill my purpose. Missing links are only in the mind of the perceiver. Same for you. When there seems to be a missing link, think again. It could mean an open space for a new idea, or the fresh and new of an old concept. Missing link? Nope, I don't think so. Think of is as..."Open Space Open Opportunity."

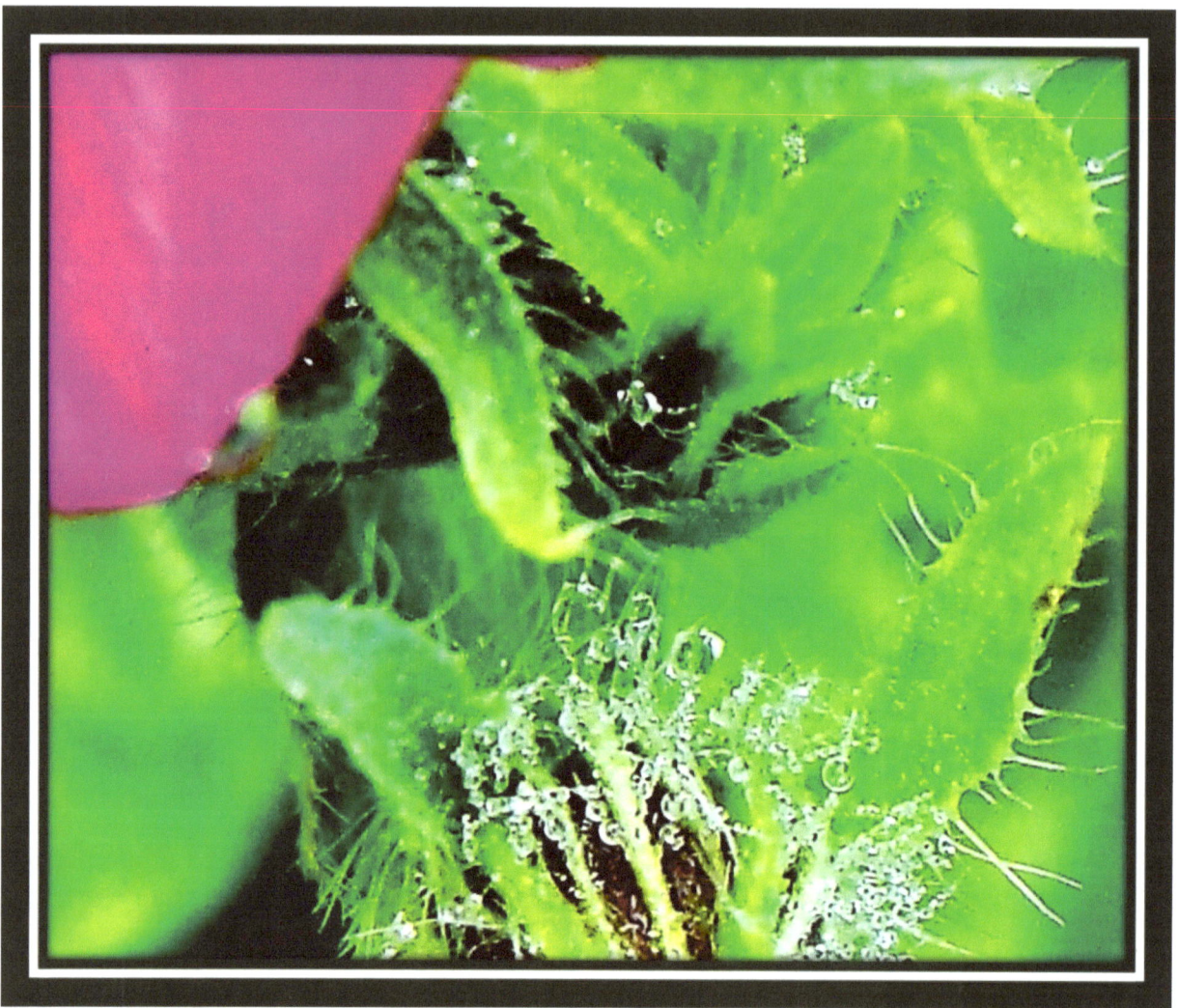

MISTY [Enhanced]

I love what I do! Surrounding the base of a flower with my misty sparking drops that glisten like diamonds of all sizes. "Ooooo, so refreshing," I hear the flower sigh. "Thank you" I reply. On occasion I'm mistaken for ice cycles by appearance, but its summer so that idea can be tossed immediately. It's a two-way street, you know, my morning job. I rest and water, the flower gives me a location to appear, and we both receive benefits from our mission. Two-way like in any relationship brings a since of belonging, intimacy, agreement, and advantage, not necessarily in that order. Being in place, and having a place to be, is part of purpose. I could think of positions where I don't belong, but that's only my imagination not my destiny. I could long to be somewhere else, but what's the use. I love what I do, and where my fate has taken me. Do you long to be somewhere else, or in a special relationship? It's always going to be a two-way street. One side must communicate with the other to meet the needs of both. It's an exciting time, getting to know one another through the stages of relationship, acquaintance, casual, close, and intimate. My advice, think two-way, try not to jump stages or things could get challenging. Take full advantage of your position in the other person's life with love and patience, and theirs in yours. Every person has special attributes. Try not to judge by previous experience. I'm sure it's not like the past, nor should it be. God created us for relationship. "Isolation is Not an Option."

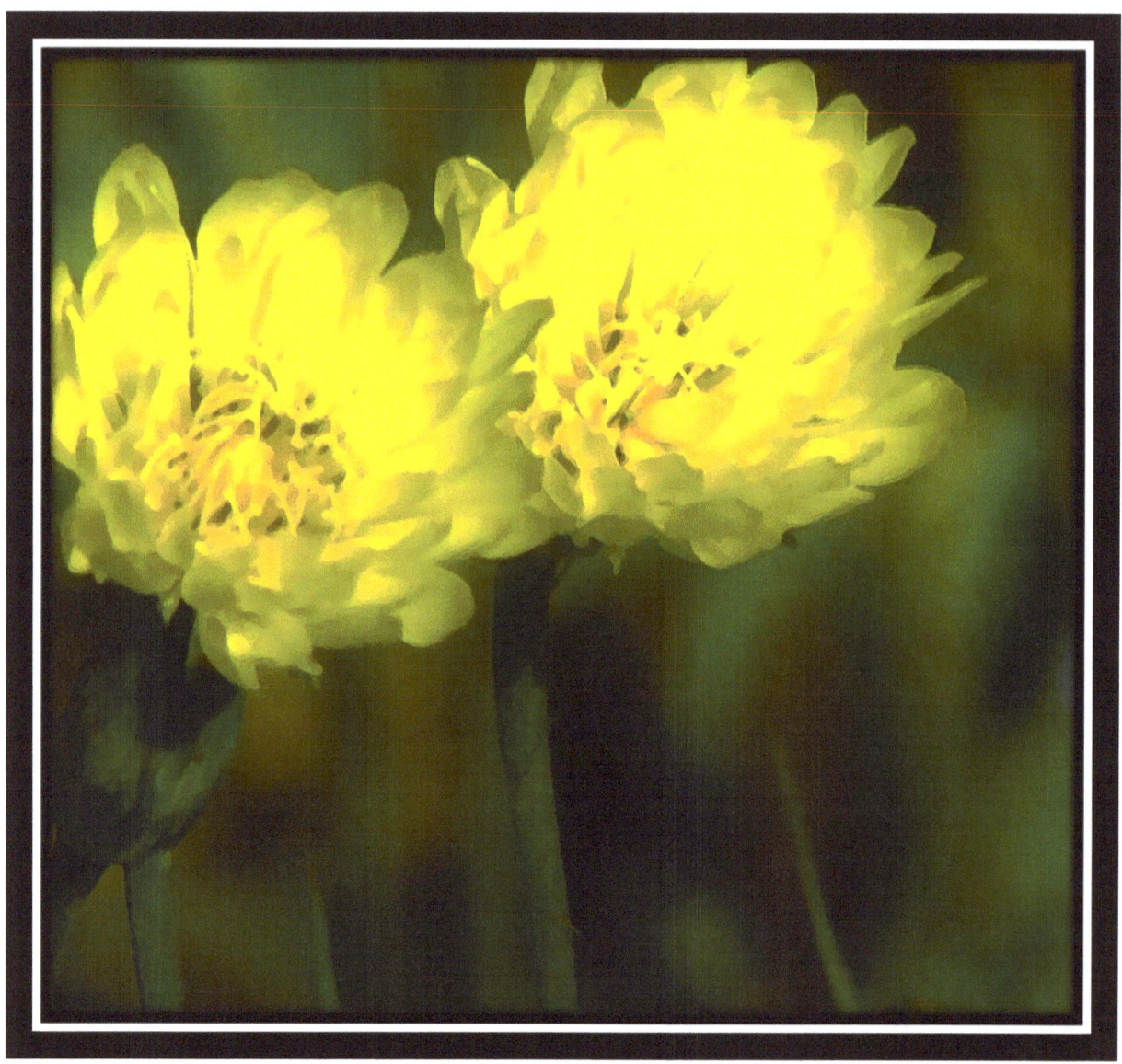

UN-IDENTICAL TWINS [Paint Strokes]

Do you think we look alike? Many pass by and say. Awww look at the identical twins. We may be similar but hardly identical. There are similarities, however, we know there are more dissimilarities. For example, our petal count is totally different, but because most only glance, they see same. Our buds are completely unalike pointing in different directions, but because most only glance, they see same. We appear as if we're leaning in the same way soaking up at the sunshine, we're not, but because most only glance, they see same. Oh not to be pegged as twins, but because most only glance, they see same. Everything and everyone has its own identity. Absolutely nothing on the planet is identical. God created every speck and molecule, grain of sand, leaf, absolutely everything with its own characteristics and DNA. It's up to you to take a closer look. See the beauty and individuality intertwined in all creation. Whether plant, animal, or human it's diverse. Maybe you should remove that deceptive term "identical" from your vocabulary. We feel it does a disservice to creativity as you begin to compare, and create measurements, pitting one against another. Take a closer look! Judgement are brutal. Perfection is expected. Take a closer look! Embrace the uniqueness of our individuality, because when you glance, you miss out and, "Only See Same."

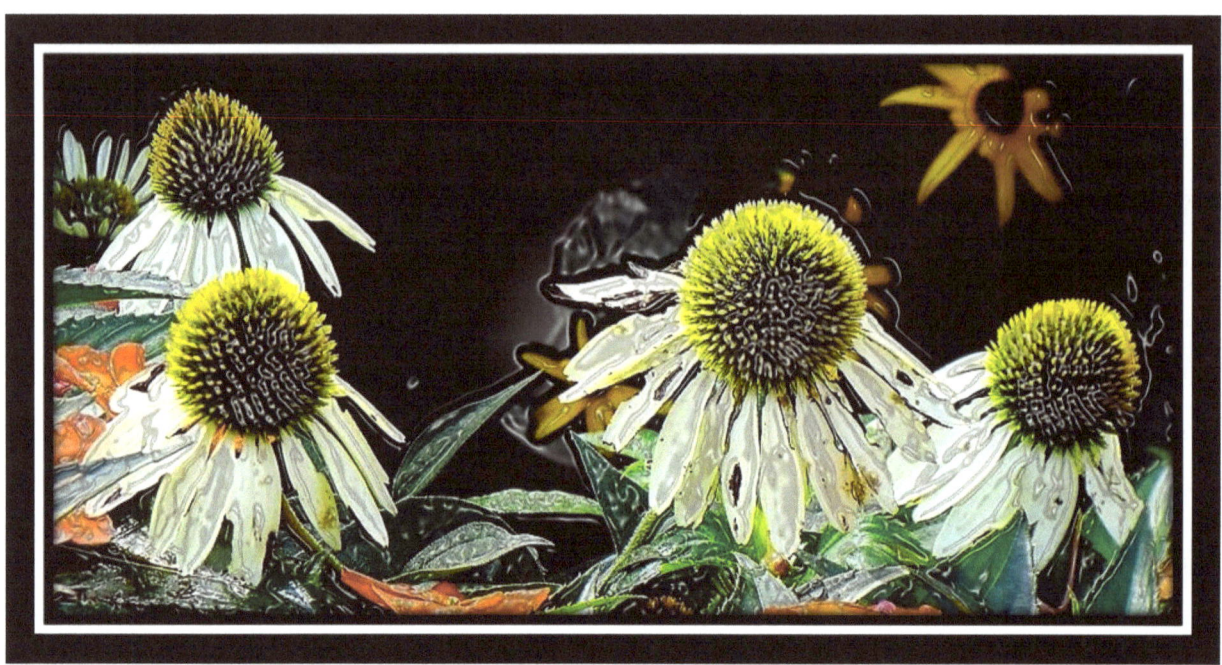

MIC CHECK [Plastic Wrap]

"May I have your attention please?" "Mic check! Mic Check!" "Can you hear me now?" "Testing testing 1-2-3." "Listen up!" "More monitor please." "Is this thing on?" "Check 1-2, check 1-2." "This is your principal speaking…" "We are beginning our pledge drive…" "You're listening to WBWC your classic music radio station." "Test 1-2, test 1-2." "This is breaking news…" "We'll give him two minutes to share…" "Thank you all for coming…" "We are having a few technical difficulties…" "These are your afternoon announcements…" "All music, all the time…" "Now we will hear a selection from our next artist…" "The next voice you'll hear…" In five minutes we will begin the program." "Our next guest will be…" "This is only a test…had this been an actual emergency…" "We'll be right back after station identification…" "There will be a teachers meeting…" "Did I put this on right…there it is?" "More volume please…" "Mic check…mic check…"

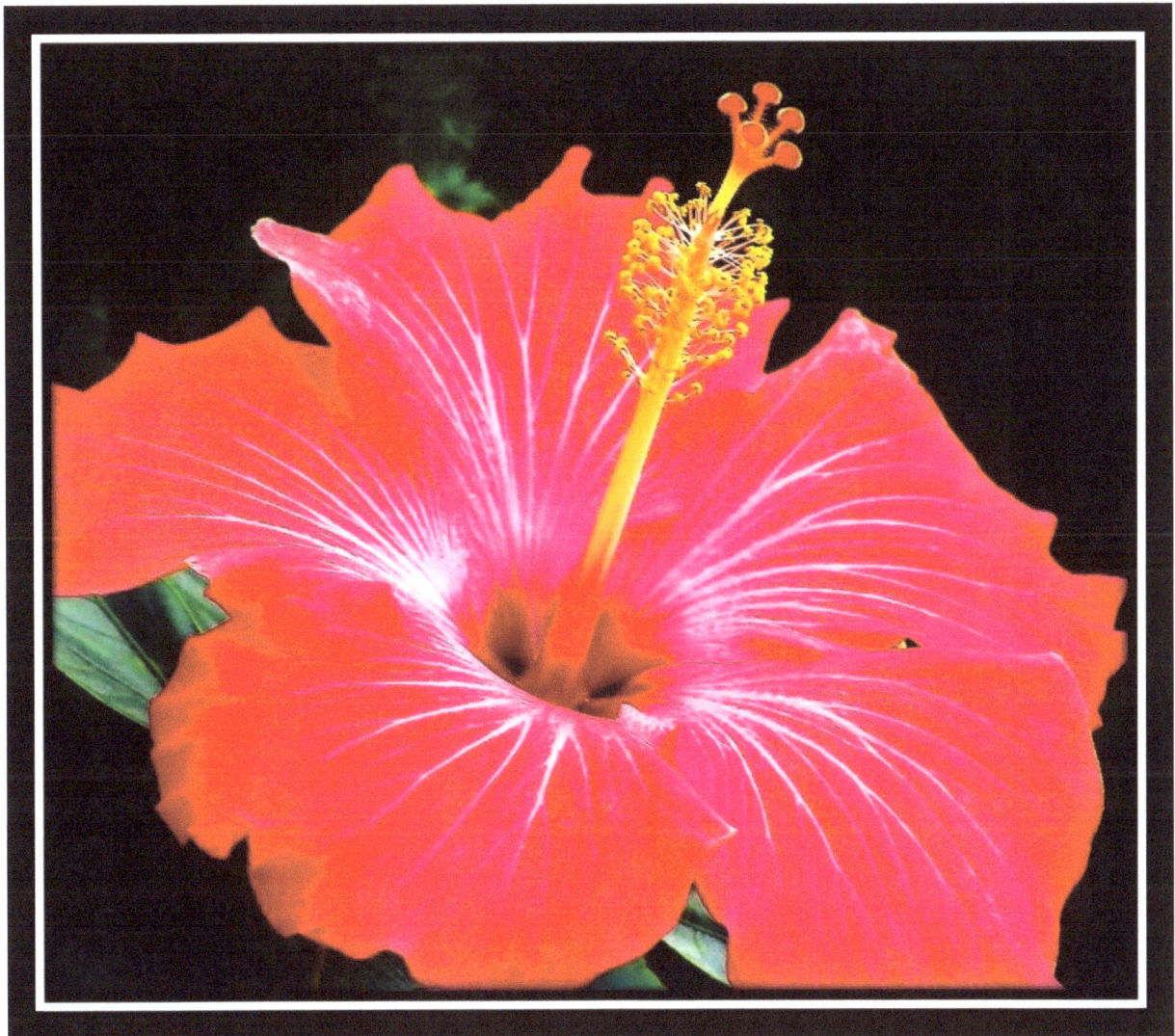

The Announcement [Enhanced]

"We're getting married!" "I'm graduating!" "I got the job!" "We got the house!" "He's my new boyfriend!" She's my new girlfriend!" "I got the part!" "I'm now a published author!" "I made the team!" "I was elected class president!" "I'm prom queen!" "I'm prom king!" "We're having our first child!" "I passed the exam!" "I'm now certified!" "I was accepted into…!" "We won the game!" "Your're invited…!" "It's my birthday!" "It's our anniversary!" "It's a boy!" "It's a girl!" "Surprise!" "The car is yours!" "We're engaged!" "I'm moving!" "We're going on vacation!" "I won the…!" "Congratulations!"

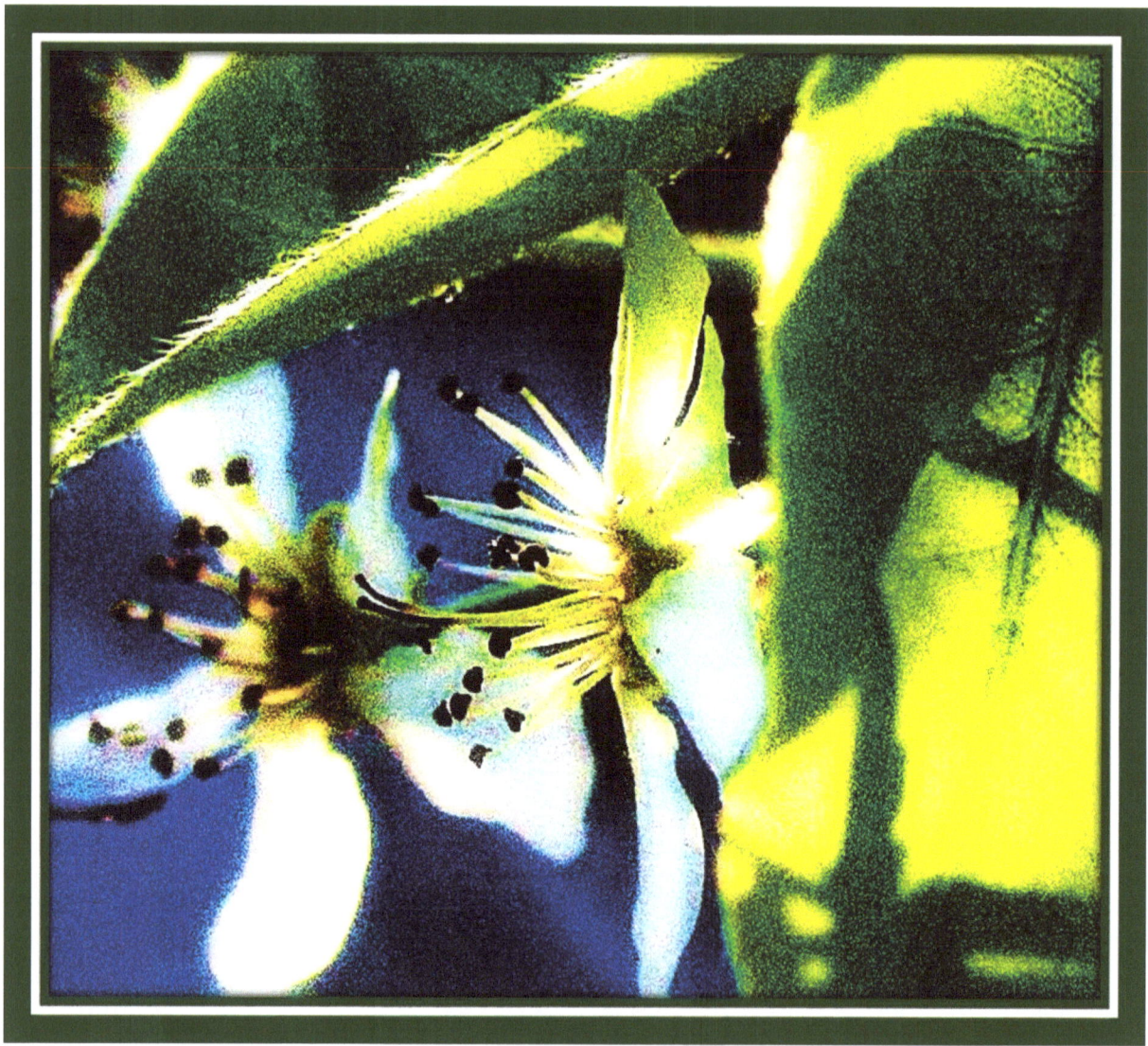

BEHIND THE CURTAIN [Glow Diffuse]

Are you ready to head out for our performance? Almost. I'm glad we're behind the curtain until ready to make that special reveal. Yeah, I don't want anyone to see me before I'm ready to show all the time and detail put into this masterful makeup. Are my petals shiny and smooth enough? What about my tips, I bought this new black polish to enhance the color. I have to be perfect! There are people in the audience that will expect it. I took a peep, and wow, I'm so nervous. I worked really hard, but it may not be enough! Suppose I mess up? Suppose the audience doesn't accept me? Suppose I forget everything? Ahhhhh! Whew! Alright it's show time. You ever feel this way? When it's time to step out into the dream, or vision God has given you? So much doubt about acceptance creeps in, it turns into an anxiety challenge. Well, so what! Do your thing! It's all good. All of the "suppose" questions that arise are only to scare you away from your destiny. Don't let your dreams and ideas turn into the "if I... could of...would of...should of..." game. Keep in mind we all have a unique creativity built within us. That special project or idea possibly doesn't exist, or is an improvement on something that already does. That's progress! That's how God does it. No need to peep around the curtain of fear in advance for acceptance. Just go for it and "Watch What Happens!"

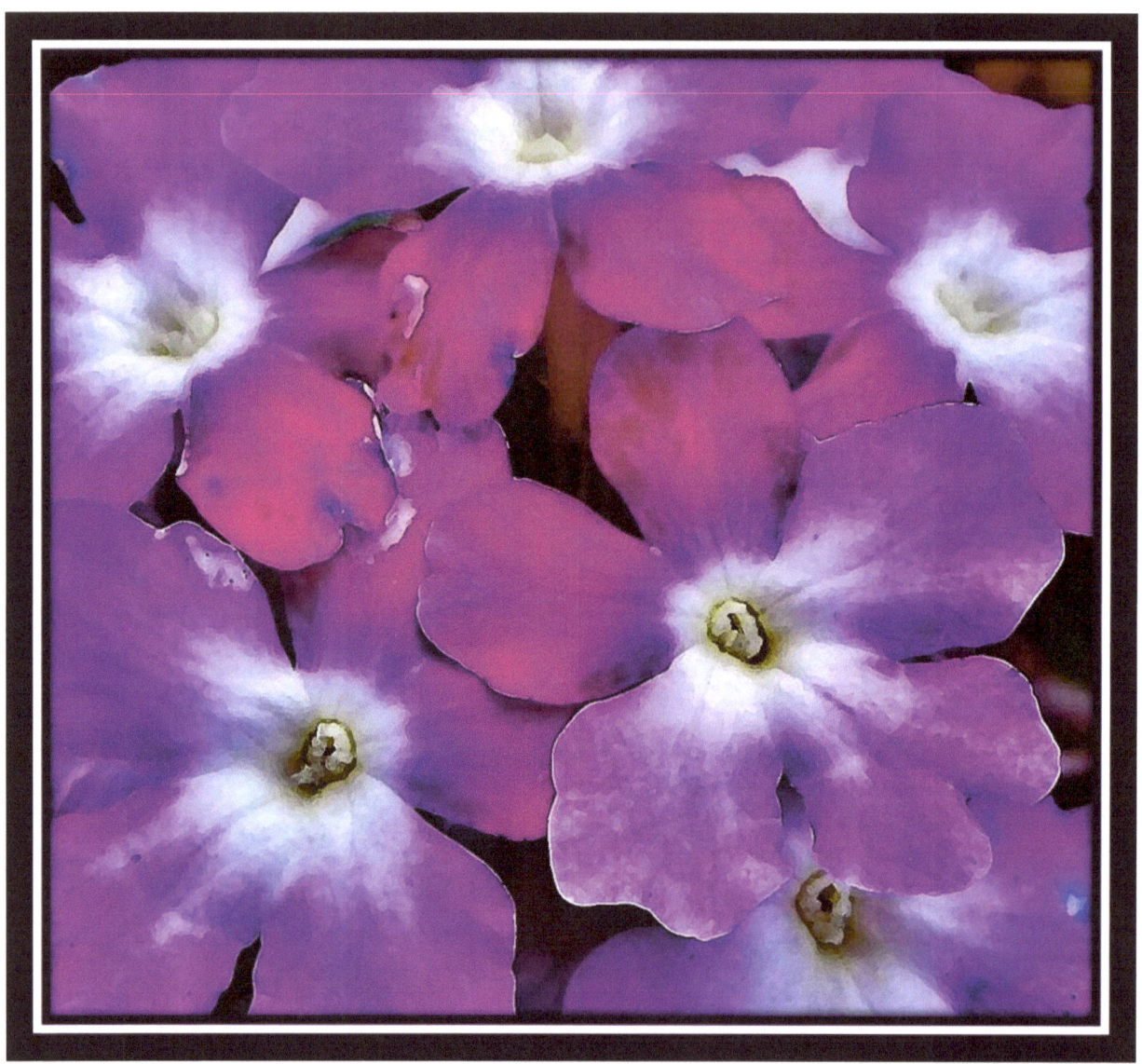

TEAM WORK [Paint Strokes]

Huddle up guys! Thank you, thank you, thank you! I think we have accomplished our goal. Although not perfect, we have come together to complete the group color challenge. I'm so proud of the work you all have done to sacrifice the petals needed to create a new color. Some struggled through the challenge, and came out with a few ragged edges, scrapes, and bruises, however, the end result, a splendid new color never seen before. Our dark brown buds and white centers still intact, light purple outer leaves still display our individual personalities, and but new color combination, awe-inspiring! You all have exhibited what the power of teamwork can accomplish! Teamwork, makes each challenge attainable. I know, it can be an inconvenience to subject yourself to the inconsistencies, and abilities of others, nevertheless, I encourage you to view teamwork in a new way. Teamwork…when your letter carrier delivers your mail, how many hands have touched it before it gets to you? Teamwork…ever been to the grocery store, and checked out an isle filled with food…how many hands have touched the item you've just purchased? Teamwork…buying gas at the gas station…making a call…cooking dinner…reading a book…taking a shower…your talents and contributions to society….etc. "And the List Goes On!"

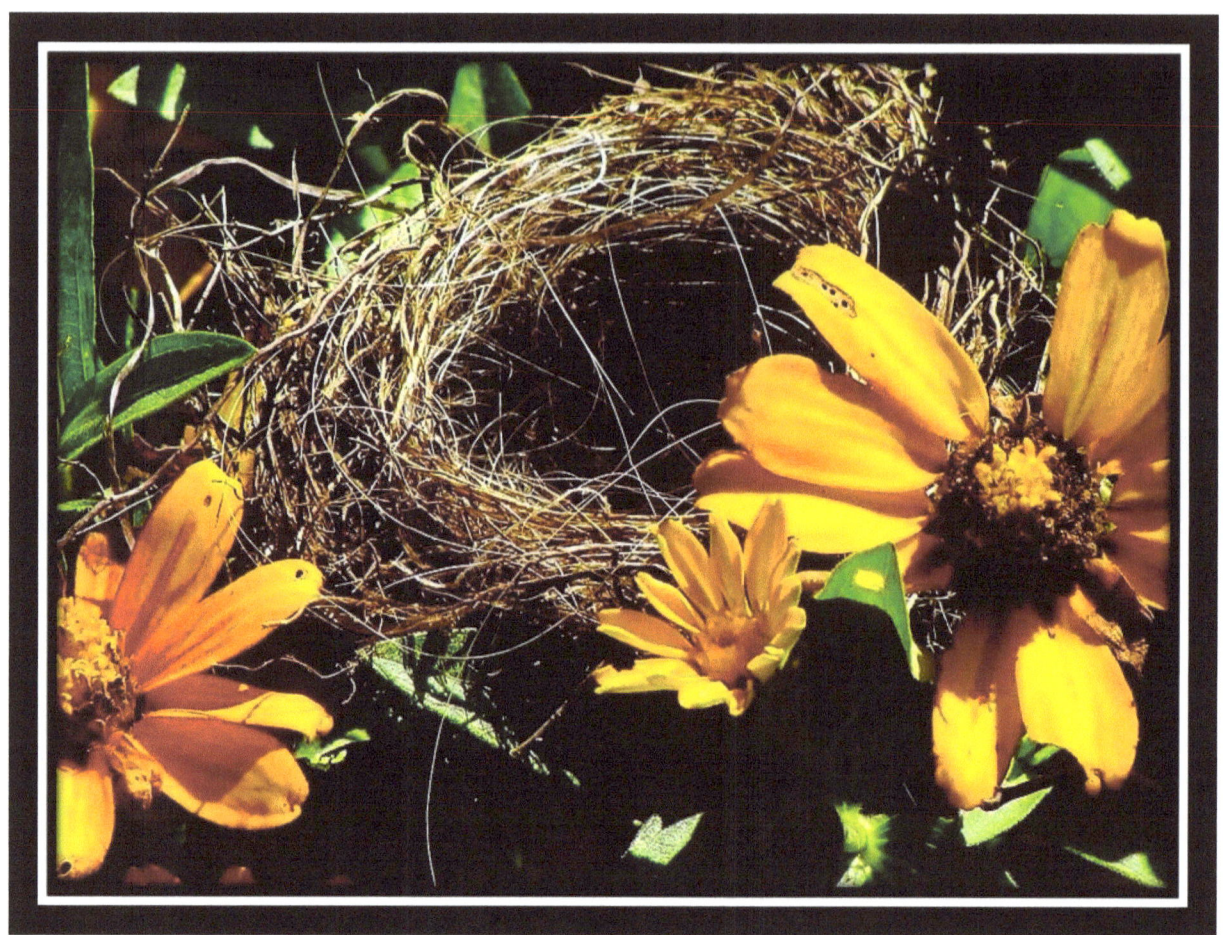

SAFE HARBOR [Enhanced]

Security! Security! I got this guys. I'm here. I've been reassigned from my normal duty to make sure nothing happens to Bird Nest. I've been deputized to step outside of my normal career of Pretty Flower, to Protector of the Fallen Nest. I never thought I would be charged with doing something completely out of my comfort zone. Wow! Suddenly I'm thrust into a position that I never saw coming! So, here I am with major responsibilities to be safe harbor, comforter and protector. It would be nice to keep a "normal" life, growing, feeling the water from the underground sprinkler, sunshine streaming through my bright yellow petals, hanging out with neighbors. Oh yeah! But now what? Bird Nest falling from his original destiny altered mine. What is "normal" anyway? Suddenly transformed, I can't believe I'm doing this. A new career that I never studied for in school, took a college course, or dreamed about. Even still, I'm going to embrace it. I'm going to allow my Creator to use me to bring safe harbor as long as needed. If I trust in the process I'll be effective. How do I trust in the process of sudden change? I'm not sure. If I do my best not to resist, allow change to bring new opportunities and experiences my way, I'll be fine… possibly. I guess nothing in our lives is totally scripted out. What an incredible story to share with my family, or one day in a biography. "From Petal to Protector," sounds like a good title to me. Seriously, you can find yourself in circumstances you never saw coming. The question is "why me?" Could be destiny. I have a journey, you have a journey, and we all have a journey, which if in our control, would be smooth sailing all the way. However, as life changes what you assumed was your original destiny, one thing I found to be helpful, take a deep breath, evaluate the situation, and walk through it with the help of God. Even if you need to take one step back you'll still be "Facing Forward."

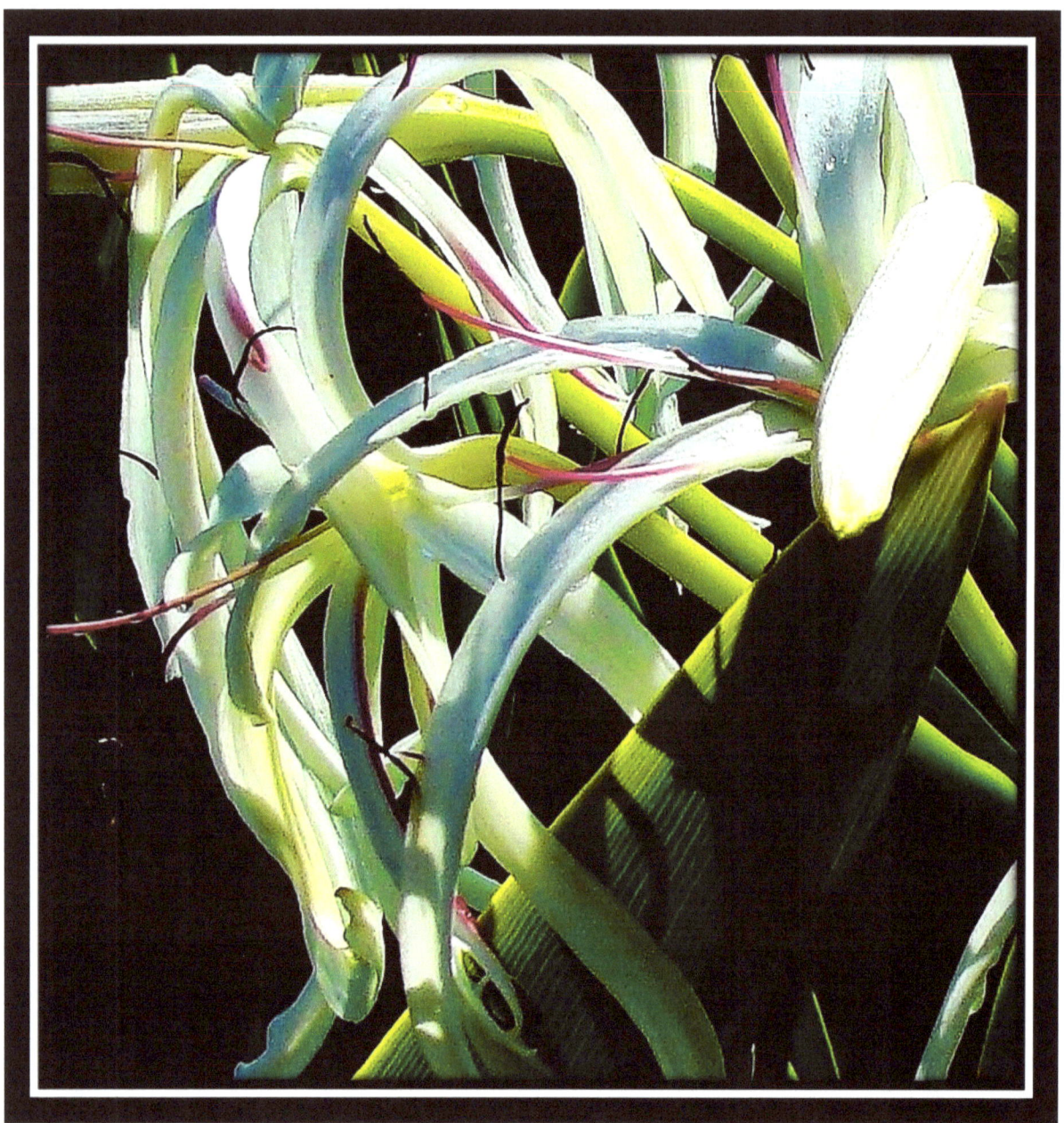

RIBBONS [Enhanced]

Don't be jealous. I'm beautiful, and yes it's a good thing I can say it. My glowing ribbons of white streaming blooms cascade down my stems, with highlights of blue, and a splash of pink, I feel lovely. I see my reflection in dew, as beach sand is rinsed from my leaves when the sun rises above the horizon of my ocean front view. I may seem like a tangled mess to those who judge, on the other hand, I'm beautiful and I feel lovely. What do you see when you look in the mirror? Beauty? A feeling of loveliness? Beauty is more than an exterior opinion. You are beautiful. You are lovely. Who sets the standard anyway? Everyone has special physical contours, attributes, and characteristics created specifically, and strategically by God to make up the "you" that is beautiful and lovely. Can you see it? To be like… never allows what belongs to you to "Shine As the Original You Are!"

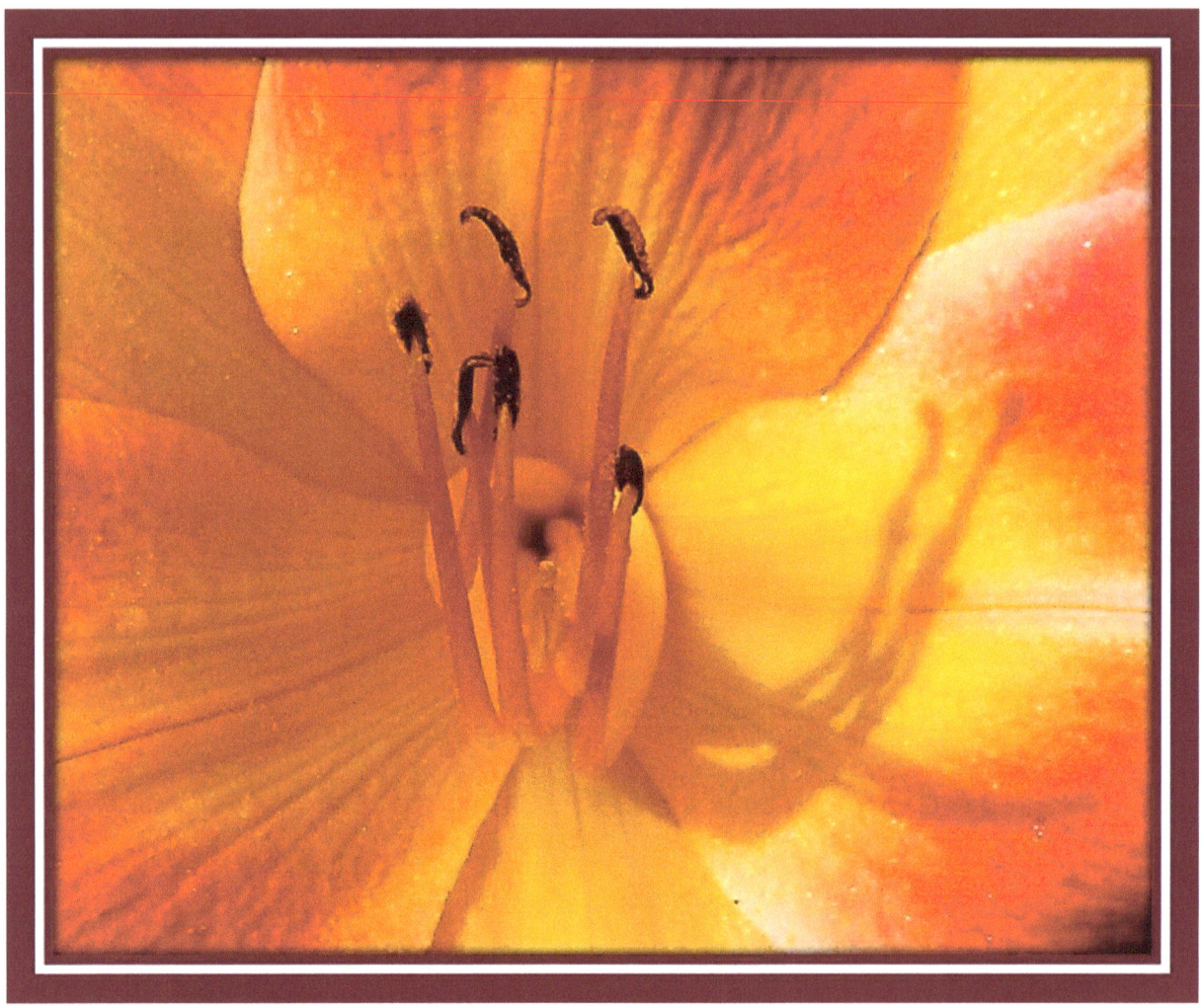

SHADOWS [Enhanced]

A perfect time of day! Perfect to see the shadows from my buds dance across my petals as the sun passes by. Time is fleeting and soon my shadows will give way to the night. Even though I'm motionless, my shadows move with the light of day. It's a good thing they don't stay in one place, their purpose is to make shade for insects, cool my overheated petals, and remind me everything must change. Some days it's hard to see my shadows when clouds cover the sun, or on a rainy day. A daily ritual I do take for granted. Like shadows, Friend-Ships pass with time like ships on the sea. They move, on occasion, like the light of day, or a sail quietly by as a ship skimming across your path. There are friends for life, rainy day friends, friends that are like clouds reducing our joy with their troubles, funny friends, activity friends, hospitality friends, giving friends, friends that pass through, and friends that stay true. Why are there so many types of friend-ships? Your heart determines every one. Some are not friends at all because you have no heart connection whatsoever, and that's okay. Everyone you meet is not destined to be your friend. God designed it that way. Personality, motivation, attitude, character, and emotion all play a role in the shadows of friend-ships. The best part is, "The Choice is Yours."

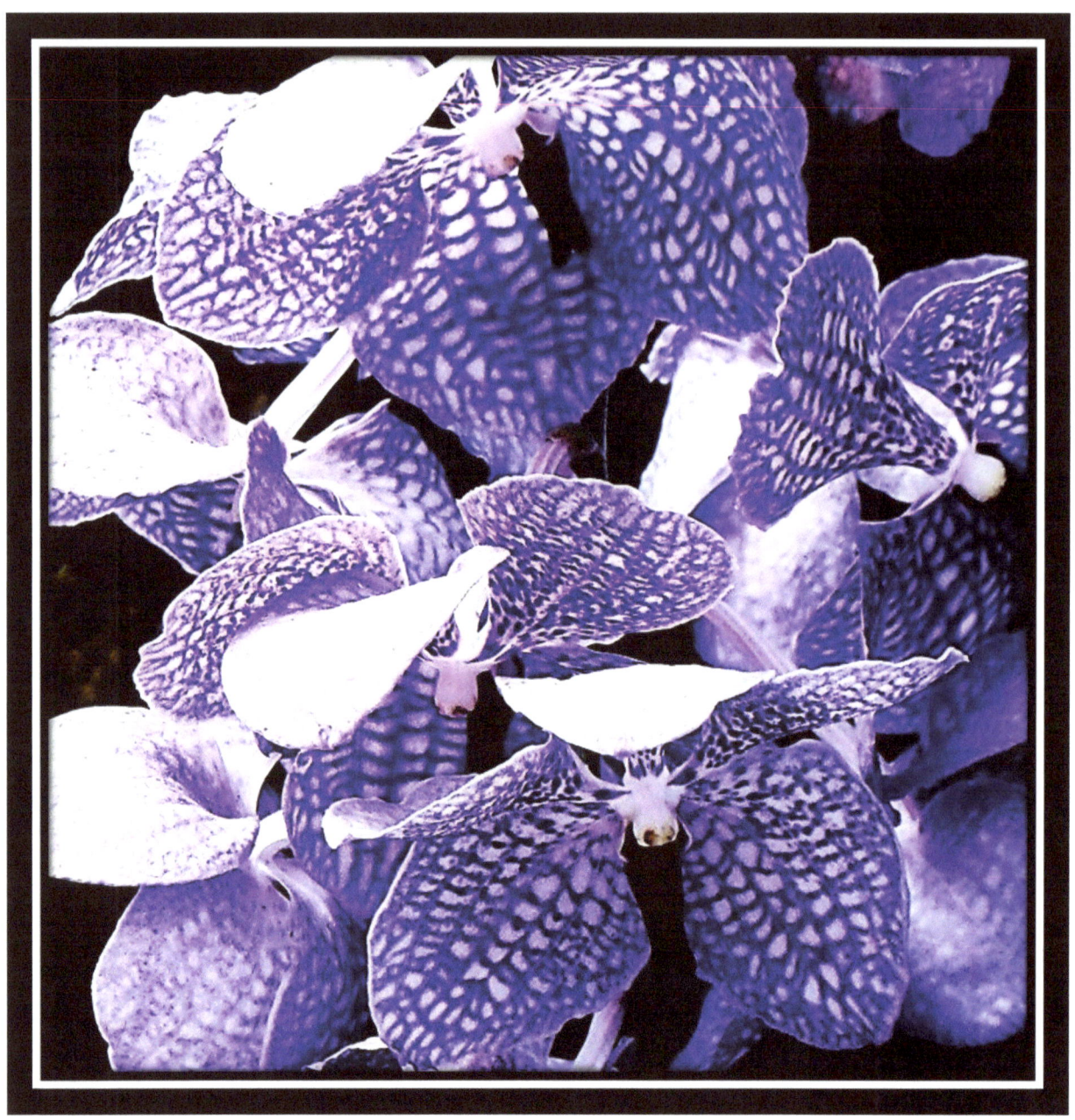

GOSSIP [Enhanced]

"Did you hear about…?" "I'm just sayin…" "Ummmmm Ummmmm…" "I'm not gossiping but…"

"Did you know…?" "Did you see…?" "I heard that…" "You know she's…" "I'm not being nosy but…" "Tell me what you know about…" "Is he still at his momma's house…?" "Girlllll…" "It was just a matter of time before…." "I saw that coming because…" "How did that happen…?" "What's going on girl…?" "I had a feeling he was…" "Did you see how she was dressed…?" "That hair baby…" "I think she had…" "Mannnn did you know…?" "Who's the girl this week…?" "He dumped her for…" "She dumped him for…" "I just want to know how to pray…" "He's got…" "I'm just trying to help…" "He said…" "She said…" "They said…" "Then I Said…"

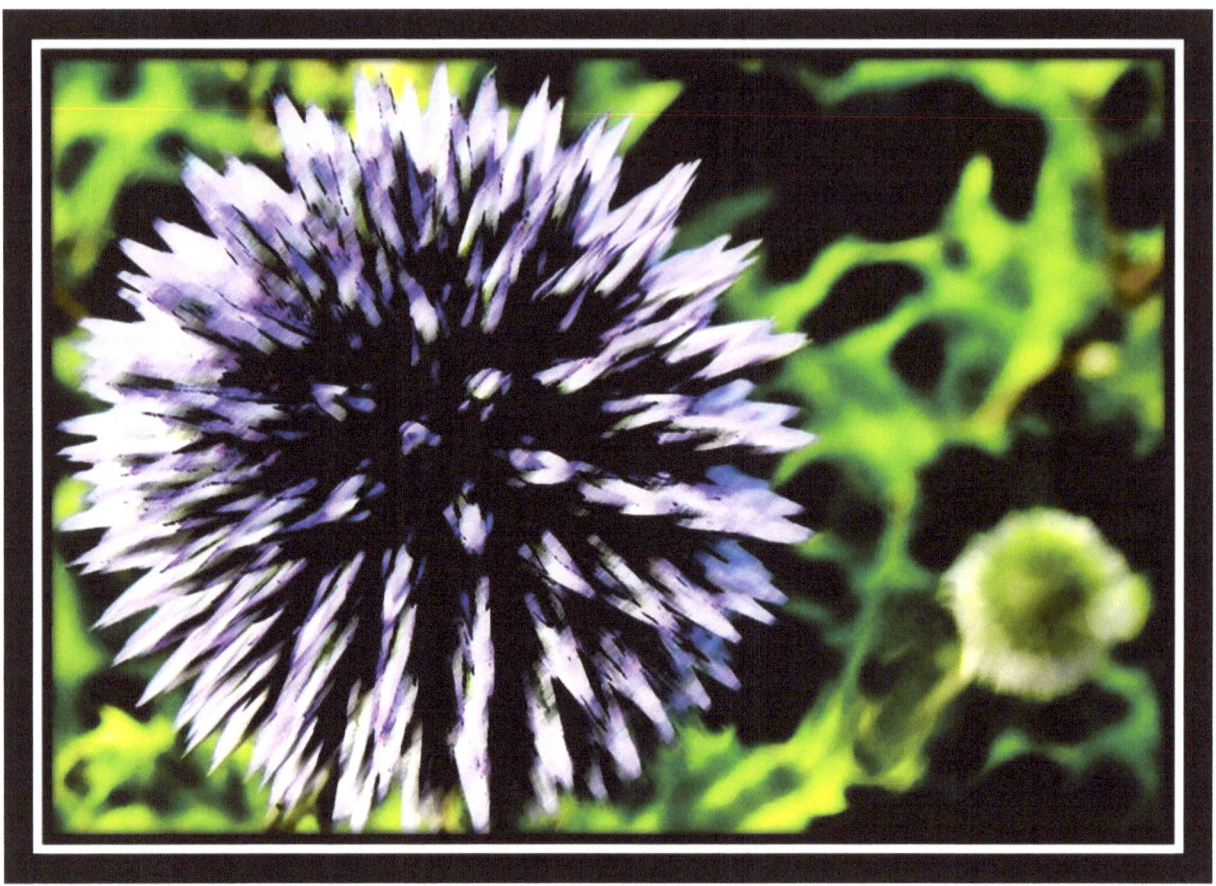

SPIKE [Paint Strokes]

Prickly, looks good on me. My spikes appear to have sharp points when, if touched, may stab the handler. Yikes! Looks are deceptive. In reality my spikes are soft as pillows, tender to the touch, and cascade from my core, which when caressed, fall without resistance. As I mature, the winds take my spikes on a premature journey across the meadow leaving me exposed to the elements. Exposure of my core is as uncomfortable as showering in public. Neighbors see my core as it really is, with all the imperfections usually hidden by my rough and tough exterior. I like it when people are afraid to come close. I like it when people keep their distance, assuming they will be injured if they touch. I feel bold and secure. What I don't like is the result. Looks create misunderstands of what really is. Are you misunderstood as a result of a rough and touch exterior? Do you really feel secure and safe, or has the deception of what lies at the core of your heart make you feel isolated and alone? Take a chance. It's probably not the horror you imagine, to allow your heart to be exposed. The hidden expressions of your heart could be a gift to others, when unwrapped and imparted. The possibilities are endless and misunderstandings reduced. To assume you are filled with imperfections is not what is. God didn't create you to be perfect, only to embrace what is..."You."

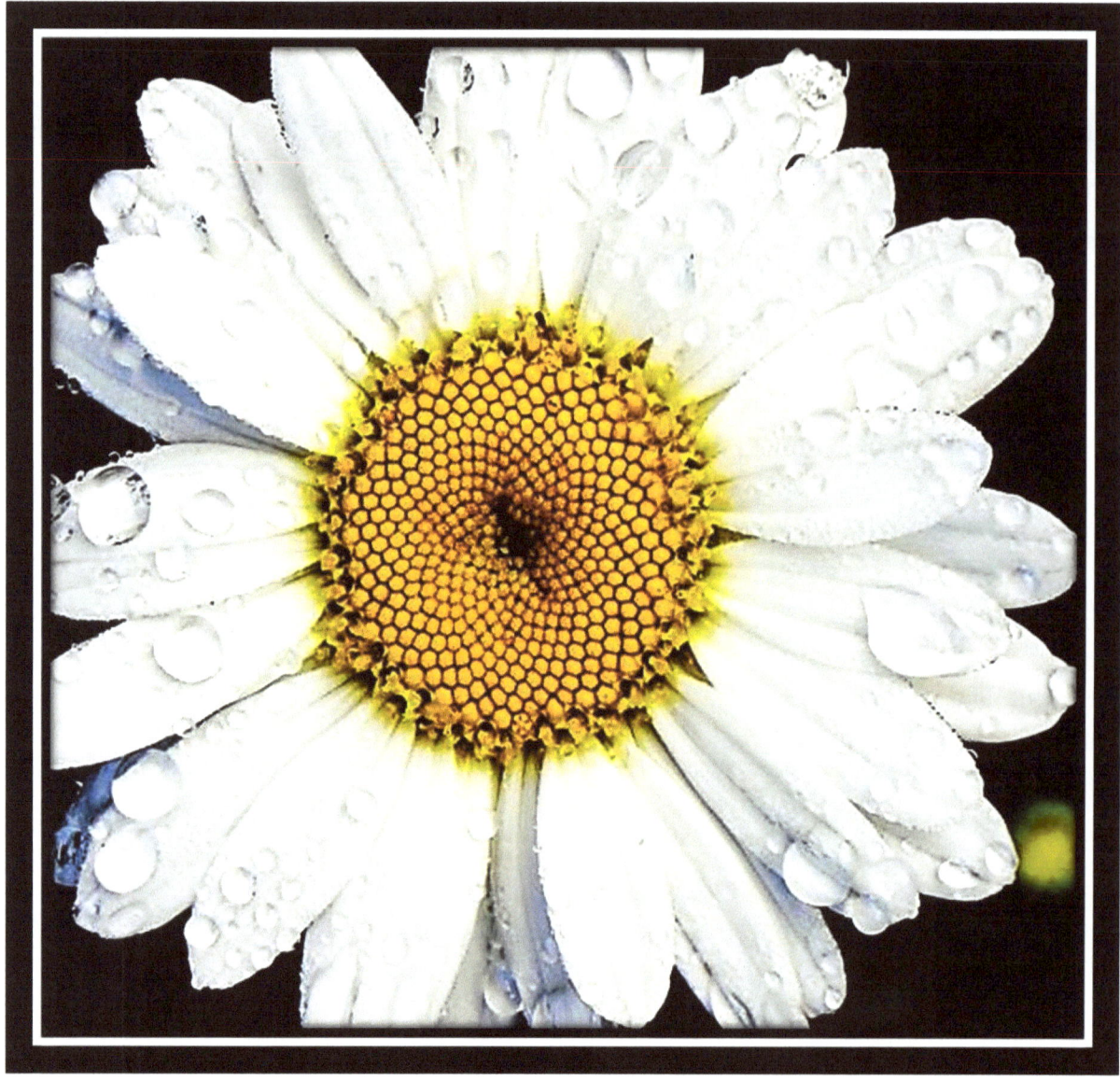

SMILE [Enhanced]

Smile! Smile! May I take your picture? Thank you! Great smile! Beauty every direction I turn. Beauty that excites me as I capture creation as it happens. Smile! I weep tears of joy to experience such splendor. I can hardly keep my battery charged. Whew! 750 pictures already! Seems like only a few snapshots. Oh well. I better download and see what exciting new details I can observe from this series. Preview once, twice, or three times, there's always new elements to notice. Maybe an insect, a drop of water, a fuzzy stem, or multicolored leaf. So much to comprehend when you take occasion to closely observe the magnificence that surrounds. Tiny specks of sand, huge boulders stacked against the ocean, a million species of fish, even the intricate design of brink and mortar in city buildings. My advice…take your eyes on vacation and smile…"Behold the Beauty of a Moment in Time."

About the Author

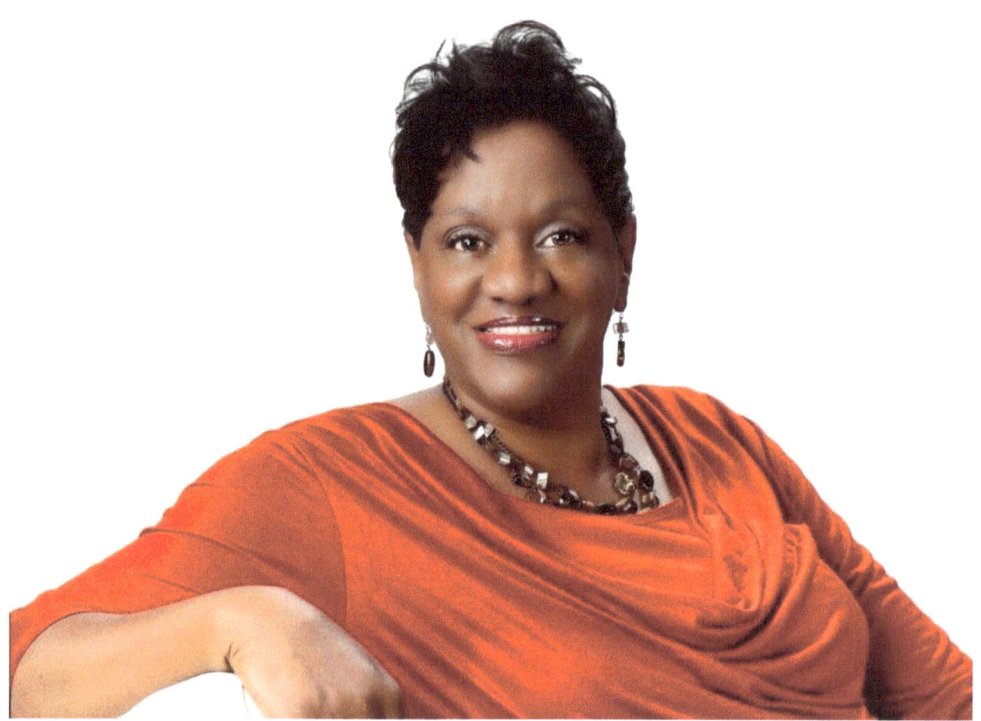

Dianne E. Woods is an Evangelist, Photographer, Author, and Purpose Coach as Founder and President of DEW Ministries, Inc. She enjoys the visual arts with a focus on nature and landscape photography. When it comes to writing her style varies, and she has published a poetry and photography work, and many self-help books. Her true passion is photography capturing creation as it happens. She finds the most challenging part of writing to be editing, editing, editing. As a mature author she hopes to let her readers understand it is never too late to reimagine your career, or move your passion from paper to productivity. Her advice for writer's young and old, be yourself, allow your work to speak from the heart, and never give up.